HANDS-ON
LATIN
AMERICA

ART ACTIVITIES FOR ALL AGES

ART FROM THE ANDES

As long ago as 1500 B.C., the Chavin, in northern Peru, created pottery covered with animal figures...especially cats. The Paracas, 3,000 years ago, wove brilliantly patterned fabrics and wrapped their dead in the yardage. The Chimu crafted goldwork that was prized by their Inca, then Spanish, conquerors. The colorful aryballo jar has stored fermented drinks for centuries. The woven dolls, alpaca clothing and wall hangings, incised gourds and crafted baskets are traditional ancient patterns but recent purchases. The art that has flourished for centuries continues today with few changes in pattern and color.

The support and interest of my sisters has contributed to the development of this book.
I have four exceptional sisters: Rebecca Richards, Martha Mortensen, Alice Ann Young and
Jocelyn Young. This book is dedicated to their appreciated encouragement.

**Book design and photography by Art & International Productions, LLC
Jim Tilly, Sasha Sagan and Oleg Parshin**

**Mary Simpson illustrated the book and
assisted in the development of the crafts**

Emily Mortensen edited the text

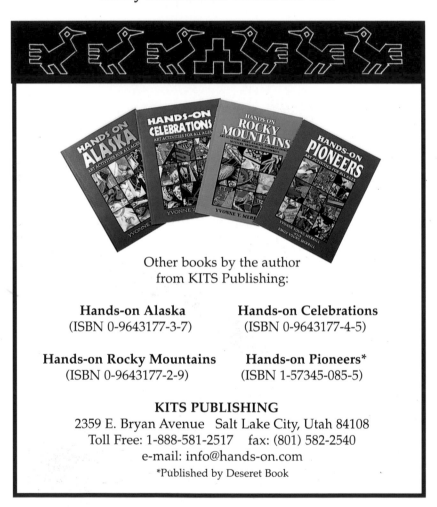

Other books by the author
from KITS Publishing:

Hands-on Alaska	**Hands-on Celebrations**
(ISBN 0-9643177-3-7)	(ISBN 0-9643177-4-5)
Hands-on Rocky Mountains	**Hands-on Pioneers***
(ISBN 0-9643177-2-9)	(ISBN 1-57345-085-5)

KITS PUBLISHING
2359 E. Bryan Avenue   Salt Lake City, Utah 84108
Toll Free: 1-888-581-2517   fax: (801) 582-2540
e-mail: info@hands-on.com
*Published by Deseret Book

© 1997 Yvonne Young Merrill

First printing October, 1997
Printed in Hong Kong

Library of Congress Catalog Number 97-69966

ISBN 0-9643177-1-0

HANDS-ON
LATIN AMERICA

ART ACTIVITIES FOR ALL AGES

YVONNE Y. MERRILL

KITS PUBLISHING

CONTENTS

INFORMATION AND TECHNIQUES THAT WILL
EASE YOUR ART PRODUCTION

This book of activities has been developed to replicate museum artifacts from ancient cultures of Central (Mesoamerica) and South America. The techniques have been carefully adapted to use available and inexpensive materials: paper, water-based paint, school glue, salt-based clay, etc. There are a few processes that recur throughout the book that give your product the essential look of *authenticity*. Often you want the look of gold and silver metal, jade, coral and turquoise, painted or weathered stone, clay, wool and linen fibers and organic dyes. Here are the formulas and materials for these effects.

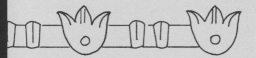 # FAUX PAPIER
Faking it with paper

Exotic gemstones
Some projects use **turquoise** (blue green), **coral** (reddish orange to deep clay red-brown), **jade** (light green to deep green), and **lapis lazuli** (royal blue), as these rich gems were widely used and are still popular in fine art objects throughout the world.
1. To create blue green, dark green, reddish brown and deep blue apply a coat of water color, tempera or acrylic paint to **both sides** of butcher paper. You can sponge on diluted greens, tans etc. to give your color a richness of authenticity.
2. After the paper has dried, spatter it with a dry toothbrush or paintbrush. **Spattering:** dip your **dry** brush into diluted brown or black paint. Flick your finger over the dry surface aiming the tiny spots of color on your prepared colored paper. Spatter here and there. Protect the surrounding areas. Spatter painting spatters everything!

Leather and burnished surfaces
Using butcher paper, manila folders, craft paper, or brown paper, cover surface with brown, rust or brown-orange rubbed-on **peeled crayons.** Make thick-colored, waxy scribbles. You may also **paint** the surface with these colors. If you have painted the paper, scribble over the dried paint with crayons. If you have crayoned, sponge with paint. Use the colors we have listed. Other treatments are:
1. Sponge strong coffee or tea over the paper in big movements.
2. Blend the crayons with your fingertips, rubbing hard. The secret of these techniques is to **blend** your media so it is hard to tell what you have used (fool the eye).

FAUX CLAY
Giving your art a look of pottery with flour and salt-based dough

Cooked Dough (self-hardening)
    1 cup salt
    2 cups flour
    4 t. cream of tartar
    2 cups **cold** water

Mix all dry ingredients in your cooking pot. Stir in cold water, mixing with your hands or a spoon. Cook on medium heat, stirring constantly until the dough looks like mashed potatoes or a firm ball This dough can be molded and will air-dry in 12-36 hours. Paint when hardened.

Mixed Dough (oven-baked)
    1 cup salt
    3 cups flour
    1 1/4 c. **warm** water

Add warm water to salt, stirring until the salt is dissolved. Add the flour and mix with your hands. Shape into a ball and use right away or store in refrigerator for one week. Cook at 250ºF. after you have formed your project. Small projects take 45 to 60 min. Paint your art form after it has cooled.

1200 B.C.
Olmec on Mexico's gulf coast are
   cultural influence in Mesoamerica.
Chavin, in northern Peru.
Golden Age of Greece

800 B.C.
Oldest pyramid in Mesoamerica built
   at La Venta by Olmec.
Chavin flourish in Peru.

600 B.C.
Zapotecs build Mount Alban in Oaxaca.

Alexander the Great

200 B.C.
Paracas, in Peru, are fine textile weavers.

IMPORTANT POINTS OF INTEREST

 # 1 Mexico City and Tenochtitlan

 # 2 Christ the Redeemer in Rio de Janeiro

 # 3 Machu Picchu in Peru

 # 4 Galapagos Islands near Ecuador

 # 5 Cotopaxi volcano in Ecuador

 # 6 Chichen Itza in Mexico

 # 7 Panama Canal

 # 8 The rain forest

 # 9 Christ of the Andes in Peru

 # 10 Brasilia in Brazil

 # 11 Angel Falls in Venezuela

 # 12 Palenque in Mexico

 # 13 Atacama desert in Chile

 # 14 Tikal in Guatemala

 # 15 Iguacu Falls in Brazil

 # 16 Silver mining in Bolivia

 # 17 Mt. Aconcagua in Argentina

 # 18 Lake Titicaca in Peru

 # 19 The Pampas in Argentina

 # 20 Tierra del Fuego

600-700
Teotihuacan destroyed, Tajin smiling
heads made. Copan, Tikal, Uxmal,
Palenque built by Maya.
Moche decline in Peru.
Tiahuanaco on Lake Titicaca in the
Andes built.
Coronation of Charlemagne

800-1000
Maya build Bonampak.
Maya Classic period ends.
Toltec take Chichen Itza.
Toltec are strong influence and build Tula.
Chimu take over Mochica river valleys
Norse villages of Vinland

1100-1200
Mixtec wars
Chimus build Chan Chan.
Cuzco founded by Incas.
Aztecs enter Mexico valley and settle
on Lake Texcoco.
Mayapan built as trade center.
Rise of Totonacs in Vera Cruz region.

1200-1492
Aztec build Tenochtitlan and conquer
neighbors
1481 Aztecs dedicate new temple by
sacrificing 20,000 Huaxtec
1466 Inca conquer Chimu captives.
Inca conquer most Andean tribes.
Maya decline.
Columbus discovers America

8

MAP OF MEXICO, CENTRAL AMERICA AND SOUTH AMERICA

1500-1572 1502 Montezuma II becomes ruler. 1507 Columbus 4th voyage, news of Spanish filters into New World.	1519 Cortes lands at Vera Cruz, burns all but one ship/Totonac ally with Spanish.	1521 Tenochtitlan falls to Cortes 1532 Pizarro lands in Peru 1542 Maya empire falls to Spanish 1572 Spanish conquer last Inca stronghold

◆9◆

NEW WORLD FOODS

Here are some of the foods that were new to the world with the Spanish conquests. Corn, potatoes, peanuts and beans were eaten daily. Dishes were flavored with cinnamon, nutmeg and vanilla. Montezuma drank cups of honey chocolate, and the Inca king may have sipped coffee. Nuts and fruits such as papayas, strawberries and pineapple were grown. The introduction to Europe of a variety of Incan potato reduced famine. The tomato and chilis, basic to many cuisines, originated in the New World. In addition, guano, a bird fertilizer commonly used by Andean farmers, doubled harvests of European farms. Many of our favorite snacks are spinoffs from these food items.

When Spanish explorers arrived in the Americas they were astonished to find mighty empires, elaborate architecture and art, magnificent engineering works and powerful religions. To the New World people, the newcomers were awesome and mysterious. Montezuma, the Aztec ruler, had received omens of pending disaster and he believed Cortes to be the king and god Quetzalcoatl, returning as foretold. The Inca leader, Huayma Capac, had been told that strange, bearded men had appeared on the coast.

When Cortes entered modern-day Mexico in 1519 and Pizarro arrived in Peru in 1532, they easily won allies and overpowered resistance. Although Aztecs, Mayas and Incas far outnumbered the invaders, the Spanish compensated with their horses and gunpowder. Since the astounded natives had never seen a horse, they first thought the horse and rider were one splendid being. Within a short time, the world of the Aztecs and Incas was destroyed, their temples razed to the ground, and their leaders murdered. The Mayas resisted until 1542. Within 100 years of the conquest most of the Mayas, Incas and Aztecs had died from new diseases brought by the invaders.

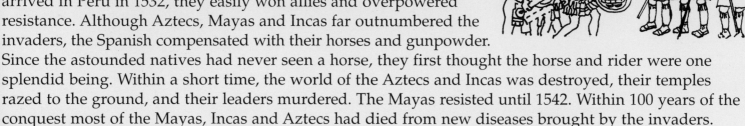

corn   beans   chocolate   potatoes   avocado   coffee   peanuts   spices   chilis

New World Influences: Foods
Though their governing power was quickly eliminated, the New World resources and knowledge forever changed the European lifestyle.

french fries   chewing gum   candy bars   soda pop   chips   peanut butter   popcorn

Prior to their introduction to the Andean and Mesoamerican cultures, Europeans ate grains, meat and a few vegetables. Grains were susceptible to pests, trampling and wind. The Incan potato became a staple alternative to grains and almost freed Europe from famine. Today three-fifths of the world's cultivated crops originated in the New World. In addition to healthful contributions, many snack food favorites would not exist without the New World foods.

Color and Cotton

In addition to the dazzle of bountiful gold and silver metals, the Spanish were impressed by the rich, red cloth in the New World. The brilliant red dye was derived from cochineal insects which fed on cactus. Cortes was so interested in the red colors he sent bags of the powdered dye to Spain. One ship transporting the powder was intercepted by the English pirate Sir Francis Drake, thus beginning the British "redcoat" uniform. Prior to the New World, European clothing was woven from linen or wool. By 1790, 3,000 bales of cotton were exported from the Americas. By 1860 more than 4.5 billion cotton bales were exported. North American mills that had once ground grain into flour became textile mills.

Rubber, Rope and Chewing Gum

Mesoamericans made extensive use of tree and plant products. Turpentine and other fuels were extracted from trees and used for heat and light. Plant fibers woven into ropes were used to wrap

construction beams together for a durable hold. Rubber extracted from trees eventually became the protective insulator for Thomas Edison's first electrical wires. We use rubber every day for tires and waterproofing. Chicle, which comes from trees, became the main ingredient for chewing gum. It was an expedition in search of chicle that first revealed the extent of Maya ruins in Yucatan.

Gold and Silver

For centuries Europe's economic system operated on a barter basis, trading goods and services but rarely exchanging coins. Then came the influx of mineral wealth from the New World. Between 1519 and 1650 the New World added 180 to 200 tons of gold and silver to Europe's treasuries. From this beginning middle class merchants, bankers and businessmen emerged as well as the coin-based economic system we use today.

Health Care and Hygiene

Compared with the New World, European medicine and hygiene habits were primitive and steeped in suspicion. The New World natives had an impressive knowledge of the human body, derived largely from human sacrifice and body dissection. Mesoamerican "surgeons" used sharp obsidian knives and were skilled in drilling for brain injuries. Herbs were used for their medicinal value. Coca leaves, which extracted cocaine, were chewed in the Andes mountains for energy and to numb body pain and cold discomfort. Every town had a *temazcallic* or public bath. Aspirin, salves and quinine for malaria were all contributions from the New World.

DESIGNER JEWELRY

DESIGNER JEWELRY

Materials: aluminum baking pans, permanent yellow and orange markers, prepared "faux" jade and coral paper, lapis lazuli and emerald gems (page 7 for instructions), floral wire, gold or silver metallic thread, scissors, any permanent markers for color designs, puncture tools such as a small nail point for embossing foil.

1. Look at our samples and other jewelry and design your jewelry piece. Start with a large circle shape, a rectangle, a diamond or a free-form triangle. The multiple sectioned necklaces are especially authentic. Draw it onto an aluminum baking surface and cut out with scissors.

2. Give the metal a gold finish before or after you cut by coloring with yellow, orange or/and permanent marker and blending with a paper towel or your finger.

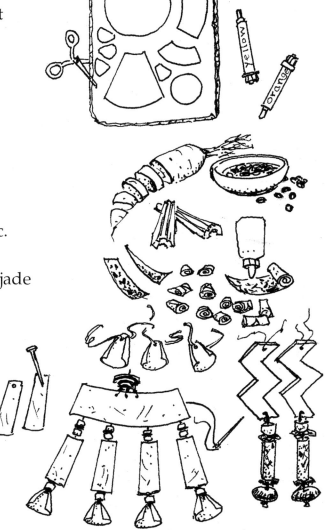

2. **Veggie jewels:** cut carrot rounds, soaked black beans, cross-sections of celery, beet parts, etc.

3. **Rolled paper jewels:** cut varying widths of jade or coral paper and roll into bead tunnels.

4. Attach parts by punching holes with a sharp tool. Attach with thick thread or floral wire.

Be imaginative with your jewelry attachments:
    *canning lids and rims make handsome
     hoops
    *cardboard and poster board can be cut into
     many shapes.

Jewelry with gold and precious stones reflected social status. Only rulers and nobles could wear jewelled headbands, lip and ear plugs, handsome knee and arm bands and stunning rings, necklaces and bracelets. Gold was worn by the upper class. Today the silver of Taxco, Mexico is a popular momento for travelers. Amethyst, carnelian opals, topaz and turquoise were much admired.

NEW WORLD RED

NEW WORLD RED

Materials: two sticks (4-6 inches long), various red yarns, red construction paper, tube pasta, red water-base paint, brush, soaked beans, canning lid, scissors, glue and beads (optional).

EYE of GOD (OJO de DIOS)

1. Cross the sticks and fasten with yarn going over and under, at center loop to firmly secure yarn and sticks. Continue wrapping yarn from arm to arm changing your reds. Tie and cut end when you are done. Tassels are optional.

AZTEC HEADBAND

1. Cut strips from the red construction paper 6"x 18", 3"x 18" and 4"x 9". Fold 6"x 18" lengthwise. Cut points along the top edges. Cut out and glue bright decorations on center of headband strip.

2. Clip fringe (feathers) on top edge of 3"x 18" strip. Cut several of these tissue strips and also clip feather fringe on the top edge.

3. Make tall center feather by shaping a 4"x 9" strip and clipping feather fringe around the edges. Repeat the shape and fringe it in about six layers of tissue. Staple tissue on either side of the construction paper feather. Glue in place.

AZTEC PENDANT

1. Paint the tube pasta. String the soaked beans, pasta and beads. Cut colored circles for the canning lid. Hammer a hole at the top. Attach to pasta necklace. Here are Aztec designs for ideas:

The Spaniards were intrigued by the brilliant red objects throughout the Aztec empire. They sent bags of the rare, red dye to Spain. It is said that the actual source of the dye was not discovered until the microscope was invented. The Dutch scientist van Leeuwenhoek examined the dye under a microscope. He found hundreds of tiny insect parts. The red dye comes from crushing the female bodies of the cochineal bug which fed on cactus farms. Today cochineal farms thrive in Spain. Cochineal is still the only red dye approved by the U.S. Food and Drug Administration. See page 76 for additional information.

AZTEC RATTLE

AZTEC RATTLE

Materials: half a manila folder, two 7 inch paper bowls, tempera or acrylic paint in white, brown, black and deep red, four yards of coordinating ribbon, scissors, pencil, glue, stapler, brushes, tongue depressor or dowel for handle and beans for rattle sound.

1. Choose a design for the center of your rattle. Prepare two pieces of manila card stock for the pop-up center figure. Draw it on one, remembering to include the 3/4" tabs for folding and attaching. Cut out the double designs.

2. Draw your design pattern ideas on scratch paper. Refer to page 79 for authentic ideas.

3. Staple the edges of the bowl together, keeping a 1" space for the ribbons and stick. Insert the beans through the space. Paint the rattle, front and back. Paint the pop-up design on both sides. Glue it together and paper-clip to secure gluing. Fold the tabs.

4. When the paint is dry, glue the pop-up tabs to the center of the rattle. Some of your rattle design might be painted onto the surface and some might be painted cutouts that are then glued. Paint or glue the designs to the rattle.

5. Cut ribbons to varying 12" lengths. Staple them together in the center. Insert the stick handle and ribbons between the bowl edges in the inch space. Glue or staple.

Music, song and dance were an important part of all ancient people's rituals. Rattles, drums, flutes, whistles, metal bells, trumpets and shells were played. Spaniards described the music as tuneless and monotonous. Aztecs made their rattles of clay, metals and turtle shells. The conch shell called people to gather in the central square for ceremonial events.

INCA PANPIPES

INCA PANPIPES

Materials: 48 inches of white, half inch PVC plumbing pipe (available at hardware stores), a saw for cutting PVC pipe, corks for plugging open bottoms, 36 inches of string, floss or yarn for aligning pipes, half inch strip of stiff material that can bend around pipes, at least 15 inches long, and a handmade weaving needle of plastic (yarn for tassels is optional).

The concept of these pipes is that your breath blowing over the enclosed hollow pipe will cause vibrations that will create a sound. It is similar to blowing over the top of an empty bottle.

1. Measure the piece of PVC pipe into 7 to 8 inch lengths following this guide:

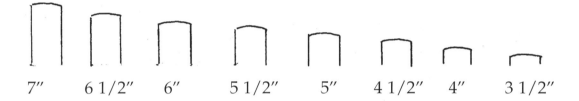

| 7" | 6 1/2" | 6" | 5 1/2" | 5" | 4 1/2" | 4" | 3 1/2" |

The shortest pipe will give you the least sound.
You may want to eliminate it.

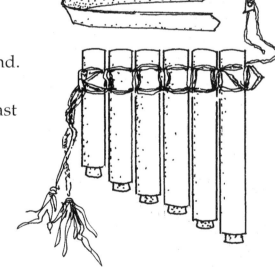

2. Plug up the bottoms of each pipe with the corks.
The fit should be tight. Blow into each and test its sound.

3. Cut a piece of stiff material, 1/2 inch wide and at least 15 inches long. It might be matte board, plastic from a milk bottle, poster board, etc. Line up the pipes from largest to smallest. Wrap the strip around the pipes creating a horizontal bar front and back. Make a pliable plastic needle (from a plastic carton) with a punched hole for an eye and weave 36 inches of string over and under the stiff horizontal bar, securing the aligned pipes in place. Add a couple of tassels of natural alpaca-looking yarn for a touch of the Andes.

Panpipes and flutes were made of hollow bird bones, condor quills, bamboo or clay. Today there are several professional groups that entertain with authentic, ancient instruments, creating the haunting sound of the Andean mountain music.

CLAY PLAY

CLAY PLAY

Materials: there are many kinds of molding materials. We have used cooked salt dough for a hard, permanent finished product. Modeling tools such as craft sticks, a toilet paper roll for the jaguar, a paper juice container for the Maya vase, brushes and your choice of paint. The recipe for cooked salt dough is on page 7.

MOCHICA STIRRUP-SPOUT HEAD CUP

1. Mold your flattened clay around an inverted plastic cup from a yogurt or Jello pack. Model the facial features. Add textured hair and cover opening with clay. Make a coil and form the stirrup over the head. Add earplugs, hatband and jewelry.

2. Cover with plastic wrap so drying will be slow to avoid cracking. The Mochicans painted their cups. Choose your colors of paint.

PLAY DOUGH VASE OR STIRRUP-SPOUT JAGUAR

1. Form the dough around a toilet paper roll or juice can. Insert small strips of meat tray Styrofoam into jaguar leg extensions that will help grip the body when you attach the legs as well as increase strength.

2. Drying will take several days. Paint the jaguar when dry.

Clay was a common material for all New World people. They did not seem to be aware of the pottery wheel, rather, they used slab and coil methods. The Maya fresco vases had encircling scenes. Aztec bowls were decorated with bold zig-zag lines. Vessels were etched, painted and stamped. Since the Incas did not have a written language, their pottery gives us important insights into their culture. Pottery continues to be a prized art form in Hispanic cultures.

WEAVING

WEAVING

Materials: assorted yarns, 4 yards of each color, cardboard strip as loom, cotton warp thread, scissors, a handcut plastic needle with large eye.

1. Decide on a wrist band or woven choker necklace, or a band for a bookmark etc. Cut your cardboard loom strip to fit the length:

      7 inches for a bracelet
      14 inches for a woven choker
      10 inches for a bookmark strip

2. Choose your yarn palette and roll yarn balls of at least 4 yards each.

3. Cut a 2 inch plastic flat needle from a milk carton. Poke an eye into its broad base. This is your shuttle for the weft which goes over and under the warp threads.

4. Mark on your cardboard strip 1/4 inches on each edge, facing you. Loop your warp thread over and under the notches.

5. Weave with your shuttle, over and under, paying careful attention with each row. Push each row tightly against the completed rows to make a tight pattern. Leave a tail of weft each time for your finished edges.

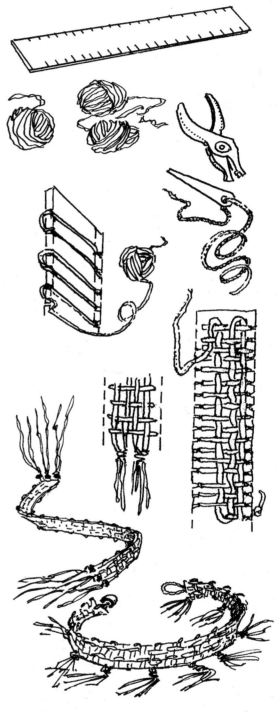

In Inca, Maya and Aztec cultures women were expected to be weavers. Men and women spun the fibers after men sheared the wool or harvested the cotton and flax. The backstrap loom was most commonly used. The pre-Incan cultures made some of the ancient world's finest woven fabrics. Woven, knitted and embroidered fabrics continue to be valued.

ANCIENT MATH

Materials: for the Codex use a manila folder, Styrofoam meat trays, scissors, pencil, black or brown acrylic or tempera paint, paint tray, coffee and sponge brush for aging the paper. For the Quipu use heavy, bright string (six or more colors), 18 inch lengths.

MAYA CODEX

1. Brush strong coffee over manila folder. Let dry. Divide and fold into four accordian pages.

2. Plan your codex book story. Make colorful drawings with markers.

3. Cut out styrofoam stamp about this shape and size.

4. With a dull pencil draw into the styrofoam stamp, but not penetrating the other side. If you want letters you must write them backwards on your stamps.

How the Mayas made numbers

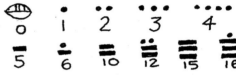

5. Paint with a brush and practice printing. When you are ready print onto your accordian pages. Print the Maya number system using the edge of a styrofoam piece and pencil eraser for bars and dots. Decorate both sides of your book.

INCA QUIPU (kwee poo)

1. Braid the three sets of string into a 12 to 18 inch braided anchor cord. Tie your number cords to it about 1 1/2 inches apart. The Incas wore their quipu as a belt.

2. Devise a code for the information you wish to record that would include color, knot numbers and the distance of knots, etc.

The Mayas, Aztecs and Incas kept records but in different ways. The Mayas used "glyphs" which is a picture that might represent a word or an entire thought. Mayas carved their records into stones called "stelaes" or printed them on handmade paper. The pages were made from plant bark and is known as *amate* or bark paper. Glyphs were painted with ink on the long strips of bark and then covered with a protective paste and folded accordian style. The Incas kept careful records of stored goods and war spoils paid in tribute with their quipus, but they did not have writing. The Aztecs used picture symbols.

STONE WONDERS

STONE WONDERS

Materials: a Styrofoam slab 12" x 18" x 1", a ruler, kitchen knife, rubber cement glue, paint, brush and an old toothbrush. Styrofoam for the arch should be at least one inch deep. Packing Styrofoam works well for both projects.

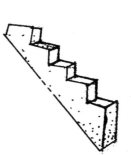

THE PYRAMID

1. Cut from a Styrofoam sheet carefully and accurately these five squares:

> an 8 inch square
> a 6 1/2 inch square
> a 5 inch square
> a 2 inch square

From the center of the 8 inch square cut out a 3 1/2 inch square.

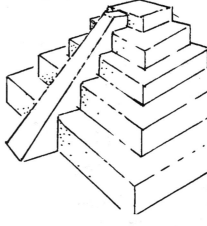

2. With two-step rubber cement, glue all Styrofoam pieces together. You have made a pyramid.

3. Decide if you want a stairway up each side or fewer. With a paper strip laid against the tiers, measure the stairway. Cut one for practice. Try it out. Improve the fit and use it as a pattern to cut the others.

4. Paint with a brush or spray paint the pyramid to resemble lime-stone (grey/white). Texturize by spattering with paint on a dry toothbrush as described on page 7.

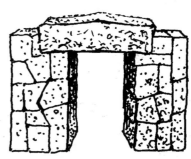

INCA STONE DOORWAY

Cut the top lintel piece to go above the doorway. It needs to be wider than the doorway. Cut the rest of the stones to fit snuggly together at sides and above the doorway. Rubber cement the pieces securely. Paint and spatter to resemble old stone as described with the pyramid.

Because these ancient people carved, built and worked with stone, we have many remains of their architecture. Temples, government buildings, storage towers, roadways and viaducts all attest to their rock-cutting skills. The giant stones that were a fort for the Incas in Cuzco were so tightly fit a knife could not be wedged between the stones.

FOLK ART OF CENTRAL AND SOUTH AMERICA

Throughout Central and South America there is a mix of Spanish and pre-Columbian influences. The culture, religion and folk art are a blend that is both unique and identifiable. The native cultures have retained their original forms and continue to present them with contemporary adaptations for festivals and celebration events.

THE MAYA

PEOPLE of the NEW WORLD

In the 16th Century, Spanish explorers in the Americas encountered three great civilizations: the Aztecs and the Mayas in Mesoamerica and the Incas along the Pacific coast in the central Andean region. The people were a conquered mix of tribes and nations. In most cases they called themselves by their indigenous name: the Chimus or Chancas in the Inca empire, the Mixtecs or Toltecs in the Aztec empire. Though they shared the physical characteristics of olive skin, dark hair and eyes, their city and empire organizations differed, their values and religions varied, their clothing was unique and their artistic expression differed.

a Maya priest/ruler   *the Aztec ruler*   *the Inca King*

the temple at Tikal   *a ruler/priest*   *a codex book*   *a warrior in gear*   *a jaguar god*

The Maya

The Maya culture was influenced by the advanced civilizations of the Olmecs which preceeded them. The Maya had impressive architecture, art and religious figures. Little is known of the Olmecs, but archeologists know the Maya had an unusual beauty code.

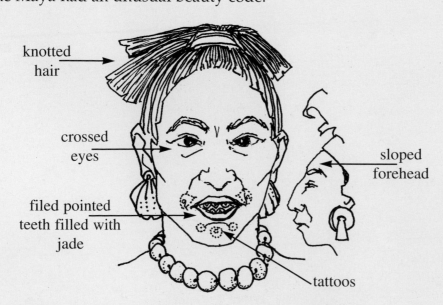

knotted hair

crossed eyes

filed pointed teeth filled with jade

sloped forehead

tattoos

feathered headpieces worn by the nobility

ACHIEVEMENTS OF THE MAYA

Astronomy

Archeologists have found observatories in most of the Maya city-states. The Maya translated their sophisticated knowledge of astronomy to a calendar by which they ruled their daily activities and religious practices. Their advanced numbering system and calendars are studied today in an effort to understand the extent of Maya knowledge.

Religion

Priests were all-important in Maya society. This powerful group determined criminal justice, taxation laws, planting and harvesting practices and temple construction. The priest carried out human sacrifice. Mayas sacrificed youth, first painting the body blue, and then feeding the victims fermented juice before weighing them down with jewels and gold. Finally they were thrown into the sacred pond or *cenote* as a sacrifice to their gods. A *cenote* was a natural limestone waterplace, common throughout the region.

Architecture

Maya ruins reveal amazing patience and knowledge of physics and stonework. Mayas had sufficient knowledge to build large structures capable of enduring.

| *carved stelae* | *corbelled arch* | *the ball court* | *a temple* |

Commerce

The Maya had a river and road system for trading, travel and communication. The Maya highlands produced obsidian, jade, flint for weapons, feathers, copal and cochineal dyes. From the lowlands came salt, cotton, honey, dried fish, wax, meat, shells, pearls and slaves.

THE AZTECS

THE AZTECS and their ANCESTORS

Like the Incas, the Aztec empire, known for its aggressive and cruel society, was a combination of several cultures which became a single power in the early 1400's. Archeologists know little about these cultures, not even what they called themselves. The names assigned to them are modern-day names used for easy reference.

The Olmecs: 1200 B.C. to 300 A.D.

The Olmec are credited for building three great temple cities. Their sculpted stone heads, as big as eight feet tall, were carved nearly 2,000 years ago and transported to hilltops, overlooking hills and roads. Little is known about their method in moving these heads or their purpose. The Olmec are believed to have invented the ball game, *tlachtili*. Discoveries indicate the Olmec painted their bodies red, blue and yellow and prized the slanted forehead. The jaguar was central to their art and design.

The Zapotecs: 500 B.C. to 300 A.D.

Little is known of the Zapotecs, but scientists have found their city, Mount Alban, which featured sewage and drainage systems, baths and impressive city planning.

The Toltecs: 900 to 1200

The Toltec culture was so revered that the Aztecs manipulated their lineage where possible to claim Toltec ancestry. Archeologists believe that the artists and craftsmen of this group enjoyed a tax-free status within their community. Toltecs are probably responsible for the great city of Teotihuacan, just outside today's Mexico City. The ancient city had a population of 250,000 and was 3 1/2 miles long and 2 miles wide. They built Tula, a trade center near Vera Cruz on the Pacific Ocean.

The Totonacs: 1300 to 1400

Cortes landed near the city of Vera Cruz where the Totonacs assisted him in finding the great Aztec capital, Tenochtitlan.

The Mixtecs: 1200 to 1400

The legend of the white-skinned god, Quetzalcoatl, originated with the Mixtecs. The story predicted the return of this powerful god around 1519, the year Cortes landed in Mexico. Montezuma, the Aztec ruler, assumed that white-skinned Cortes was the returning god.

The Aztecs: 1200 to 1521

The early Aztecs were nomadic traders, regarded by existing cultures as primitive, inferior "dog eaters." Aztec religious practices were demanded by their god *Huitzilpochtli* who struggled every twenty-four hours to again cause the sun to rise. His energy for this cosmic effort came from the blood of sacrificed fresh hearts. There were four central gods in the Aztec belief system:

PEOPLE of the NEW WORLD

In the 16th Century, Spanish explorers in the Americas encountered three great civilizations: the Aztecs and the Mayas in Mesoamerica and the Incas along the Pacific coast in the central Andean region. The people were a conquered mix of tribes and nations. In most cases they called themselves by their indigenous name: the Chimus or Chancas in the Inca empire, the Mixtecs or Toltecs in the Aztec empire. Though they shared the physical characteristics of olive skin, dark hair and eyes, their city and empire organizations differed, their values and religions varied, their clothing was unique and their artistic expression differed.

a Maya priest/ruler   *the Aztec ruler*   *the Inca King*

the temple at Tikal   *a ruler/priest*   *a codex book*   *a warrior in gear*   *a jaguar god*

The Maya

The Maya culture was influenced by the advanced civilizations of the Olmecs which preceeded them. The Maya had impressive architecture, art and religious figures. Little is known of the Olmecs, but archeologists know the Maya had an unusual beauty code.

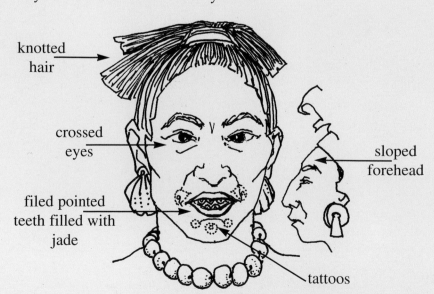

knotted hair

crossed eyes

filed pointed teeth filled with jade

sloped forehead

tattoos

feathered headpieces worn by the nobility

ACHIEVEMENTS OF THE MAYA
Astronomy
Archeologists have found observatories in most of the Maya city-states. The Maya translated their sophisticated knowledge of astronomy to a calendar by which they ruled their daily activities and religious practices. Their advanced numbering system and calendars are studied today in an effort to understand the extent of Maya knowledge.

Religion
Priests were all-important in Maya society. This powerful group determined criminal justice, taxation laws, planting and harvesting practices and temple construction. The priest carried out human sacrifice. Mayas sacrificed youth, first painting the body blue, and then feeding the victims fermented juice before weighing them down with jewels and gold. Finally they were thrown into the sacred pond or *cenote* as a sacrifice to their gods. A *cenote* was a natural limestone waterplace, common throughout the region.

Architecture
Maya ruins reveal amazing patience and knowledge of physics and stonework. Mayas had sufficient knowledge to build large structures capable of enduring.

carved stelae   *corbelled arch*   *the ball court*   *a temple*

Commerce
The Maya had a river and road system for trading, travel and communication. The Maya highlands produced obsidian, jade, flint for weapons, feathers, copal and cochineal dyes. From the lowlands came salt, cotton, honey, dried fish, wax, meat, shells, pearls and slaves.

THE AZTECS

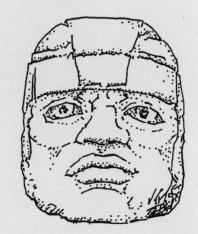

THE AZTECS and their ANCESTORS

Like the Incas, the Aztec empire, known for its aggressive and cruel society, was a combination of several cultures which became a single power in the early 1400's. Archeologists know little about these cultures, not even what they called themselves. The names assigned to them are modern-day names used for easy reference.

The Olmecs: 1200 B.C. to 300 A.D.

The Olmec are credited for building three great temple cities. Their sculpted stone heads, as big as eight feet tall, were carved nearly 2,000 years ago and transported to hilltops, overlooking hills and roads. Little is known about their method in moving these heads or their purpose. The Olmec are believed to have invented the ball game, *tlachtili*. Discoveries indicate the Olmec painted their bodies red, blue and yellow and prized the slanted forehead. The jaguar was central to their art and design.

The Zapotecs: 500 B.C. to 300 A.D.

Little is known of the Zapotecs, but scientists have found their city, Mount Alban, which featured sewage and drainage systems, baths and impressive city planning.

The Toltecs: 900 to 1200

The Toltec culture was so revered that the Aztecs manipulated their lineage where possible to claim Toltec ancestry. Archeologists believe that the artists and craftsmen of this group enjoyed a tax-free status within their community. Toltecs are probably responsible for the great city of Teotihuacan, just outside today's Mexico City. The ancient city had a population of 250,000 and was 3 1/2 miles long and 2 miles wide. They built Tula, a trade center near Vera Cruz on the Pacific Ocean.

The Totonacs: 1300 to 1400

Cortes landed near the city of Vera Cruz where the Totonacs assisted him in finding the great Aztec capital, Tenochtitlan.

The Mixtecs: 1200 to 1400

The legend of the white-skinned god, Quetzalcoatl, originated with the Mixtecs. The story predicted the return of this powerful god around 1519, the year Cortes landed in Mexico. Montezuma, the Aztec ruler, assumed that white-skinned Cortes was the returning god.

The Aztecs: 1200 to 1521

The early Aztecs were nomadic traders, regarded by existing cultures as primitive, inferior "dog eaters." Aztec religious practices were demanded by their god *Huitzilpochtli* who struggled every twenty-four hours to again cause the sun to rise. His energy for this cosmic effort came from the blood of sacrificed fresh hearts. There were four central gods in the Aztec belief system:

Quetzalcoatl
the feathered snake

Huitzilpochtli
the hummingbird

Tlaloc
the rain keeper

Coatlicue
mother of all

AZTEC ACHIEVEMENTS
The Calendar
The Aztec calendar included 18 months, each having its own sacrifice festival. They feared the world would end every 52 years. The Aztec also used a numbering system and pictograms to record trade.

Tenochtitlan
According to Aztec mythology their hummingbird god showed his "chosen" people where to settle. The sign was an eagle perched on a cactus with a serpent in its beak. In 1325 they built their great city on Lake Texcoco, hiring the Toltecs and other artisans to beautify it.

The Chinampas
The Aztecs built chinampas by layering mud and swamp plants until an "island" existed. Trees were planted whose roots secured the floating plot. These were gardens with connecting canals for canoe passage.

The Aztec Market
Spaniards marveled at the great variety of goods sold at the weekly market.

THE INCA

Before the Incas

What we know as the Inca empire actually evolved from various groups whose ancestry dates back thousands of years. The empire expanded until 1438 when all the pre-Inca cultures merged into one, bringing their remarkable strengths and achievements into a single empire. Pre-Inca cultures shared the following characteristics which were refined under the central Inca rule:

*highly organized governments
*complex social systems
*economic programs
*specialized craftsmen
*religions with many gods
*adequate agricultural systems

By 1438 these cultures were brought together and restructured under the Inca empire.

THE PRE-INCA PEOPLE

The Chavin: 3, 000 B.C.
This group is famous for their pottery, often featuring the cat. From this era forward the cat reappears in succeeding Inca art and design.

The Paracas: 2, 000 B.C.
This culture is known for having created some of the finest textiles ever loomed. Their mummies are wrapped in well-preserved shawls, turbans and yards of cloth.

The Nazcas: 1, 000 B.C.
This group is famous for the mile-wide fanciful creatures etched in the ground in high mountain plateaus. The etchings were not discovered until the airplane was invented and people had a birds' eye view from Andean heigths. The Nazcas ability and purpose in etching these animals remains a mystery.

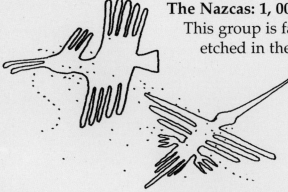

The Mochicas (Moche): 750 A.D.
These builders of a great civilization are famed gold workers, builders of aqueducts, cities, bridges, roads and canals. Their pottery is decorated with artful humor, brilliant color and the unique stirrup handle. The whimsical animals and cartoon-like scenes continue to charm collectors.

The Tiahuanacos: 900 A.D.

The famed gate to their lost city depicts a stone god at the carved center whose tears are evident. The city is in the high Andes on Lake Titicaca where many of their descendants still live. The traditional reed boats continue to be made and used.

The Chimus: 1,000 A.D.

Because the Chimus lived at the remote northernmost point of all pre-Inca cultures, they retained their identifiable handicraft style. Their gold work, skilled weaving and feather pieces were remarkable art forms. The pervasive Inca control had little impact on their art. The Spanish prized and preserved the artifacts they collected from the Chimus and considered them rare and priceless objects.

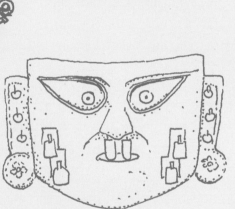

In the 14th century Chan Chan, the center of this civilization, was influential for centuries for its ceramics, jewelry and woven goods. By the 1300s they had succumbed to the all-powerful Inca, who skillfully brought in their own bureaucratic institutions while co-opting the defeated empire's leadership.

The Incas were not creators of their great Peruvian civilization, but rather the organizers of what was already established.

The great achievements of the Incas were the extensive paved roads that extended throughout their empire, their constructions, their strong and flexible bridges and the welfare system of stone towers that were found every few miles containing food and clothing for travelers in need. Their strong central government and regional officials gave the empire a stability that allowed for impressive public works, built by the subjects of the empire.

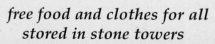

10,000 miles of roads

great stonework

bridges

free food and clothes for all stored in stone towers

Jaguar Masks

JAGUAR MASKS

Materials: a paper bag that will fit over the head comfortably, tempera or acrylic paint in orange, brown, black, white and red, a brush, water, paint plate such as an old pie tin or Styrofoam meat tray, scissors, stapler, paper punch and string.

FLAT PAPER MASK

The pattern for this mask is on page 74. Copy it for each person. Paint the mask their preferred orange and make the jaguar spots.

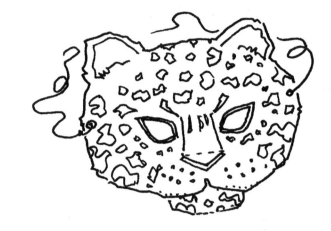

2. Cut along the dotted lines for the eyes and the nose. Paper punch the string holes. Attach the string for fastening.

PAPER BAG JAGUAR MASK

1. Cut the bottom from a paper bag until it fits the wearer's head. Pencil mark where the eyes and mouth should be cut. Draw the mouth and teeth and cut out the symmetrical eyes, mouth and nose.

2. Paint the entire paper bag your chosen color mix of Jaguar orange. Dry your jaguar on an upturned tissue box or paper towel roll.

3. Using the inside support to push against, paint the spots on the mask, using your own design. Paint the black whiskers, nose and forehead markings. Cut the white teeth and staple them in the under mouth.

4. Carefully cut out the ears at the top of the bag and fold them up. Cut a double red tongue. Staple it to the under jaw so it sticks far out of the mouth.

El tigre (the jaguar) has always been feared and respected in ancient Maya and Aztec cultures. Jaguar robes were worn by warriors. Shields were covered with the hides. Statues for worship, vessels and jewelry often depicted the jaguar. Just as in pre-Columbian times, jaguar masks are worn today in parades and festivals. Wearing the jaguar acted as a bridge between the known, natural world and the spirit world of this respected, feared animal.

THE LLAMA

THE LLAMA

Materials: a manila folder, scissors, brown paint or shoe polish, gold wrapping paper, glue, alpaca colored yarn, gold marker or crayon. For the papier mache llama you need a paper towel tube, 2 small paper tubes, tape, flour and water equally mixed to a paste, brown paper, brown yarn and bright colored ribbons or yarn (optional). Pattern on page 74.

THE SMALL LLAMA

1. Copy the book pattern, enlarging or reducing your llama. Place on the fold of manila folder, tracing around it and cutting it out. For the gold llama use marker or crayon to color the head gold.

2. Assemble the double head and glue, splaying the ends that will glue into the body slot. Glue head upright in the slot you have cut.

3. Glue on the fringed gold paper or the cut, natural colored yarn. Add a colorful bridle of bright, thin yarn or narrow ribbon.

THE PAPIER MACHE' LLAMA

1. Divide the towel tube into sections: 2 inches for the head, 4 inches for the neck and 6 inches for the back. Halve two small tubes split down the middle and tightly rolled. Tape and fit into four holes made in the cardboard tube of the llama body. Tape in place.

2. Tape all parts securely with masking tape strips. Form the ears and tail with triangles of tape. At this point you can rub with brown shoe polish or proceed to papier mache'.

3. Cut strips of newspaper, brown paper, etc. about 1/2 inch. Dip into a paste of 1/2 cup flour and water. Press the wet strips between your fingers to remove excess water. Wrap the wet strips over the entire taped animal. Let the figure dry overnight. Brush paint or sponge paint and add fringed paper for the coat and a yarn or ribbon halter.

Llamas have always been essential to the Andean people. They carry loads, and provide wool, hides and meat. Alpacas and vicunas are smaller and renowned for their fine wool. The Sapa Inca ruler only wore the butter-colored woven cloak of the vicuna. Vicunas and guanacos are wild today and range from the central Andes to Tierra del Fuego in Argentina.

THREE JADE MASKS

THREE JADE MASKS

Materials: prepared jade and coral paper as described on page 7, small cardboard tube cut in half crosswise, baked salt clay mix combined with green food coloring (recipe on page 7), scissors, glue, black, and gold paper, manila file folder and stapler. Pattern on pages 76 and 77.

TALL JADE HAT MASK

1. Copy the pattern on a manila file folder. Cut it out. Trace the face part on your choice of paper and cut it separately from the hat part. Glue to folder cardboard.

2. Trace the tall hat on your spattered jade green paper. After you have cut it out, mount it on the cardboard and on top of the face mask. Glue or staple the nose in place.

3. Cut out the decorative elements: eyebrows and hat designs.

4. Cover the cardboard tubes with gold paper, inside and outside of the tubes. Insert into earring holes. Cut out the mouth and eyes. Attach a string if the mask is to be worn. Mosaic mask continues on page 77.

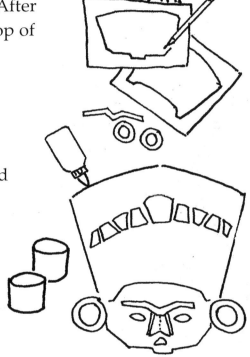

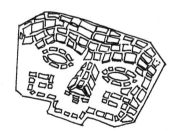

All New World people prized green stones. Jade was associated with water, the life-giving fluid and color of unripe corn. Jade was often worn as a nosering or earring. Many Maya nobles filed their teeth to a point and had jade stone inlaid in the front teeth. Masks of precious stones were made to be displayed but not worn. Intricate masks were commonly placed over the mummy bundle to protect the deceased from dangers in the afterlife.

CARVED IN STONE

CARVED IN STONE

Materials: any flat Styrofoam sheets or packing Styrofoam, a kitchen knife, paint, brush, old toothbrush, pencil and rubber cement.

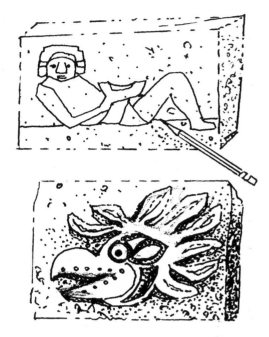

1. Look at the design on page 79. You may get some ideas for your sculpture subject. Borrow a book from the library on the art of the Maya, Incas or Aztecs. Our styro-sculptures were inspired by their stoneworks.

2. Cut your Styrofoam block. It should be at least one to two inches deep. Draw your design on a piece of scratch paper. Place it over your Styrofoam. Puncture into the foam some dotted guidelines or draw through the paper onto the Styrofoam.

3. Cut around your pencil lines with your knife placed at right angles with the Styrofoam. Then cut around your right-angle cuts with the knife blade flat to make your design have a relief look. A table knife is sharp enough for Styrofoam cutting.

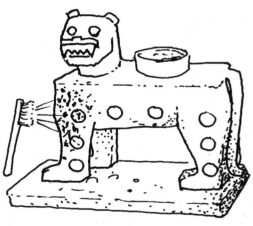

4. Cut away all the background material. Your relief image should be clean and clearly cut. Try to cut some high and low places: eyes and nose high, chin, cheeks and forehead lower, and the neck even lower.

5. Paint your carved foam any color you wish. Make it look old by spatter painting it. Dip an old toothbrush into a contrasting paint such as white, gray, black or brown and run your finger over the painted bristles, directing your brush about 8 inches from the figure. Protect your surfaces as the paint will spatter everywhere.

Maya and Aztec stone sculptors created phenomenal works of art. They created temple relief designs, funeral masks, jewelry, containers and vessels that were objects for ritual. The famous reclining figure, the Chac Mool, holds a dish that received sacrificial organs as does the vivid orange jaguar. There are many versions of Chac Mool throughout Maya art.

INCA GOLD MASK

INCA GOLD MASK

Materials: aluminum tooling foil or baking pan (a 13 x 13 inch pizza pan is good). Permanent markers of orange and yellow, prepared jade spatter paper (see page 7), various beads, canning lids, scissors, paper punch, paper towel, needle and strong thread, a nail point for piercing canning lid earrings. The pattern is on pages 76 and 77.

GOLD LEAF MASK

1. Trace and cut out the pattern on baking pan or foil. Trace around the 7 pieces with a dull pencil. Color the entire surface with yellow and orange marker, rubbing with a paper towel to create a gold surface. You may have to experiment with this step.

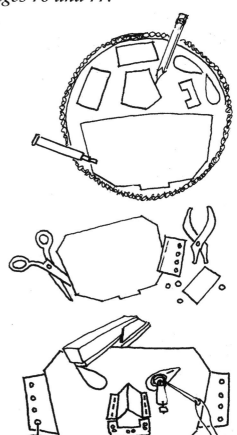

2. Cut out the separate parts with scissors. Be careful to not tear the aluminum. Punch decorative holes in ear attachments.

3. Staple on nose and almond eyes. Carefully cut out eye holes if the mask is to be worn. Assemble beads, jade paper, needle and thread for attachments. Cut jade pendants and string them through the nose. Carefully use a nail point to puncture designs in canning lids. Tie lids into ear holes.

FACE-SHAPED FOIL MASK

1. Cut two mask shaped pieces of heavy aluminum cooking foil about 12 inches square. Color the top shape with yellow and orange marker and rub as you did for the Inca mask. Press the foil onto the face, molding it over the nose, cheekbones, eye sockets and lips. Decorate with colored tissue paper, and designs from page 79. Cut out the eyes and mouth and attach with strings.

Incas called gold the "sweat of the sun". They created gold jars and statues and collected the gold work from conquered people like the Chimus, who made these golden arms. Only upper-class Incas could possess gold. Gold was given as a tribute to the sun god.

A Crocodile Mask

A CROCODILE MASK

Materials: a white paper strip 6"x 16" for teeth, 12"x 18" heavy paper (poster board or or manila file folder), markers, crayons, packing "peanuts", pencil, glue, scissors, stapler and tape. The pattern is on page 75.

1. Enlarge the pattern and transfer it to your choice of heavy paper. Color the crocodile with lots of scaly texture using crayon, oil pastels, paint or a combination of all three.

2. Cut your packing "peanuts" into 3/4 inch sections. Squeeze the peanut tops into points. Glue two sections onto nose for nostrils and the rest onto the forehead as bony plates.

3. Fold along the marked dotted lines at the head side. Clip cut lines and tape, glue or staple into place at dotted lines.

4. Cut teeth strips. Attach on each side of the mouth. The teeth should be jagged and uneven. Staple them in place.

5. Hold the mask up to your face. Mark where the string should go and where you should make eye holes. Cut out the eyes and attach the string.

The devouring crocodile was a respected creature in the tropics of Mesoamerica. Crocodile motifs appear in jewelry and headdresses for warfare.

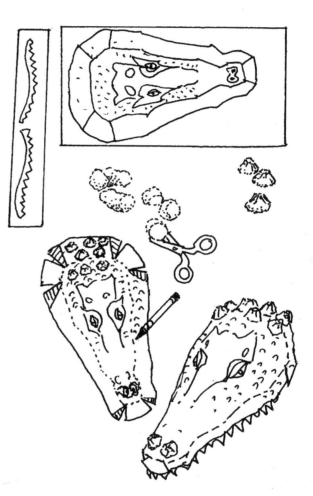

a stone carving

a feather shield

a head piece

Peruvian Cat Bag

PERUVIAN CAT BAG

Materials: a large brown grocery bag or brown craft paper, graph paper with 1/4 inch grid, three colors of yarn, markers or crayons, pencil, scissors, glue, needle and thread.

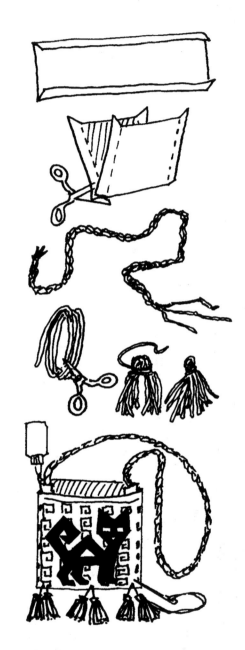

1. Cut brown paper strip 7"x 14". Fold over each long side 1 inch and then fold the whole strip in half. On each side of the center, fold and snip one inch on each side.

2. Prepare the strap and tassels. Braid three pieces of yarn into a 26 inch long strap. Wrap, clip and tie the yarn to make tassels.

3. Choose a weaving pattern for your bag. Using graph paper, color in your woven pattern. Make a cat design referring to page 79 for ideas (cats were a favorite of these cultures). Draw, color, cut out and glue your cat onto the front of the woven pattern paper. Glue the two layers to your prepared bag front.

4. Lay several inches of braided strap under the 1 inch fold on each side of the back of your bag. Glue it in place. Make a 1 inch fold on each side of the front of your bag so it fits around the back. Glue each side. Complete the bag by carefully sewing or stapling the tassels to the bottom.

Cats had symbolic religious importance to many people of early America. From 1000 B.C. to A.D. 1532 the Chavin, the Moche, the Nazca and the Chimu all used cat symbols in their art. The famed stirrup vessels of the Chavin often featured the cat. The Incas wove beautiful objects depicting cat-like figures.

SANDPAPER PRINT

Materials: coarse sandpaper (150 fine), crayons or oil pastels, colored construction paper, newsprint, glue, an old iron (or laminator press).

1. Look at these designs. Refer to page 79 for more authentic design ideas. The more complicated the design, the larger your sandpaper piece should be. Cut your sandpaper to go well with your design. Decide if this sandpaper print has a special purpose such as a greeting card or something you might frame, etc.

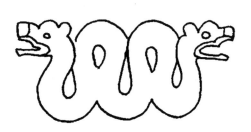

2. Draw your design. Work it out on scratch paper with a pencil before you use your crayon on the sandpaper. Press very hard and put quite a bit of wax on your sandpaper. Try to completely color the sandpaper.

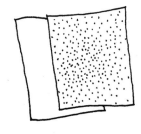

3. Place the construction paper on top of the colored sandpaper. Put a doubled paper towel or plain newsprint on top of the paper and sandpaper. Iron a corner. Lift it to make sure the iron is not too hot (blurring the colors) or too cool (not enough crayon transfer). Iron quickly. Don't leave the hot iron on the print any longer than 3 to 5 seconds. If using a laminator, place your print between newsprint to protect the press.

4. Choose your background paper and glue the print on it with a border showing.

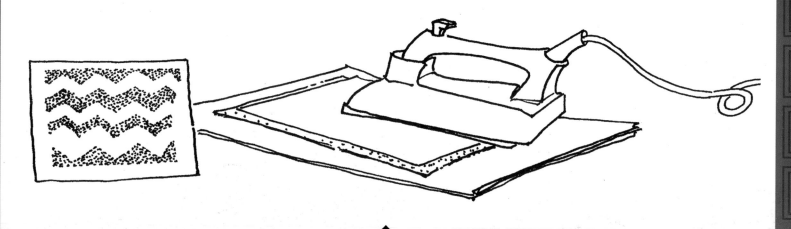

AZTEC FANS

AZTEC FANS

Materials: two salad or dinner-sized paper plates, colored tissue or contruction paper in red, yellow, black, green, pink and blue, scissors, stapler, glue, 1/4" dowel for handle, markers or crayons and bright feathers (optional).

1. Assemble your choice of paper plates. Decorate the small top plate by dividing it equally into six parts and drawing lines with bright markers or crayons. Cut a colored circle and draw an Aztec-inspired design or Aztec creature with colorful lines. See page 79 for ideas. Glue it to the center of your top plate. Here are some additional ideas for the circle.

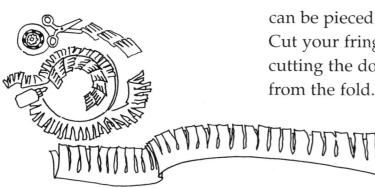

2. To make the paper fringe measure your colored paper to form a strip 36 inches long and 6-8 inches wide. Fold it in the middle lengthwise. The strips can be pieced if you can't get the continuous 36 inches. Cut your fringe from the outside toward the fold cutting the double papers about 1/2 inch away from the fold.

3. Glue or staple the inserted fringe between the nesting paper plates. Your fringe can go completely around the circle or leave a gap at the handle.

4. Glue a row of bright red paper fringe to hide the rim of the top plate.

5. On top of this outside layer cut colorful paper "feathers" of black, red, yellow, green, pink and blue (see colored photograph). Glue them on in an overlapping design. Glue the decorated salad plate over the feathers and red fringe. Insert the handle at the bottom. Insert and glue the tips of the bright feathers between the secured plates.

The Aztecs loved rich color. They found it in flowers, precious stones and exotic bird feathers found in Montezuma's royal aviary. Dahlias and zinnias filled the palace gardens. Feathercrafters used feathers from parrots, macaws and the quetzal bird with its 24 inch long green tail feathers. They created pictures, headdresses, shields, capes and fans. The feather shield that Montezuma gave Cortes when they first met was his own prized possession.

ANDEAN HATS

ANDEAN HATS

Materials: black, white or brown butcher paper, tempera or acrylic watercolor paints in black, red, blue-green and any other colors, bright markers, glue, pencil, ruler, stapler and scissors. For beaded hat: yarn, ten beads, 3/8 inch or larger needle, a nail for punching holes.

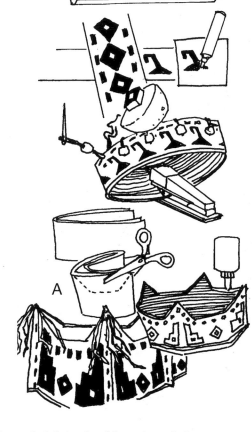

BAND HATS

1. Cut 2 strips of paper 4 1/2" x 24" to 28"(depending on the head size of the wearer) and 3 1/2 " x 24" to 28". The narrow strip will be the glued-on lining. Fold over 1/2 inch along the top and bottom margins of the wide strip. Study the Inca designs on page 79 and pencil in your pattern.
2. Decorate strip with stenciled or stamped Inca designs and glue lining to the back of decorated strip. Weight down with books until dry.

BEADED HAT

1. Do the previous steps #1 and #2. Punch holes 2 inches apart and attach each bead with needle and yarn.
2. Circle head with hatband and staple ends for a good fit.

FOUR CORNER PEAKED HAT WITH TASSELS

1. Cut two strips of paper 9 "x 24" to 28". Keeping strips together fold in half twice. Measure

peaks equal distances, mark and cut. See drawing A.
2. Pencil in your design ideas.
3. Cut a potato design. The circles can be large and small carrot ends. Crescents can be celery ends.
4. Prepare your paint tray. Brush the paint onto your veggie stamp or press it into the paint. Try it out on scrap paper. When you are ready, print your hat design.
5. Match the peaks and glue the lining to the back. Weight with books. When it is dry you are ready to attach tassels.
6. Make four yarn tassels, each 6 to 10 strands and 6 inches long (see tassel drawings on cat bag activity on page 49).
Make a row of staples at each peaked corner. Staple a tassel to each peak.

All members of the Inca Empire had a specific headwear that marked their region. One was a simple woven band of color. Others looked like woven wool bowls on top of the head. Others were dome shaped, some were woven with the familiar ear flaps or adorned with corner points. Hats were worn at all times. If you visited out of your region, it was easy to identify you by your hat. Inca officers might then inquire about you.

POPULAR ART AND HANDCRAFTS TODAY

Travelers to Mexico, Central and South America delight in the progressively creative handcrafts that are available. To some the continued preservation of the ancient crafts is gratifying. Many appreciate the adaptation of traditional materials to new design ideas or new materials to ancient patterns. The charm and practical use continue to prevail. Silver and tin are fashioned in a variety of styles, painted and natural ceramics and carved wood in whimsical forms are prized. Woven and embroidered natural fibers have brightened daily wear and festivals since the earliest of depicted events. The influence of pre-Columbian cultures is easily identified in today's craft and art pieces.

Our knowledge of Mesoamerican and Incan civilizations is a result of their legacy of fine art and remarkable crafts treasured worldwide. Today much of the art is still produced. Many craftsmen have equalled the skill of their ancestors and successfully adapted old techniques to contemporary materials such as plastic, polymer clays and new textiles.

Weaving and Spinning

Woven textiles from ancient Peru are among the finest in the Americas. Because much of their climate was dry desert, the weavings were spared the damaging effects of moisture and are often intact and still brilliantly colored, even after hundreds of years. Cotton and cactus fibers were woven by Mesoamerican women. Andean women wove wool, alpaca and vicuna (for royalty). While the women wove, men were responsible for making cordage and shearing the animals. Cotton was worn by the upper classes in the New World.

the stirrup vessel   *an etched piece*   *the aryballos jar*   *a figurine*

Pottery

The remains of decorative vessels from the New World cultures are convincing proof that the art was rich and varied. Potters did **not** use the potter's wheel, but rather the slab and coil method. Objects were painted, stamped or carved. The finest pottery was used for rituals and by the rich. Because the Incas had no written language, their pottery is an important clue to their daily lives. The peculiar shape of the aryballos jar is unique to the New World as is the stirrup vessel. Clay figurines reveal clothing, jewelry and features of New World people.

Feathercraft

Feathers from tropical birds were skillfully woven into garments and headpieces of all New World peoples. Maya priests and nobles wore tall, elaborate hats with bamboo frames. Rich Aztecs wore feather cloaks. The brilliant green feathers of the quetzal bird were worn **only** by royalty and were considered more valuable than gold or silver. The feathered serpent head is a common motif in Aztec and Maya design.

Metalwork and Precious Stones

The Peruvians had been crafting metal for 3,500 years before Pizarro collected his ransom for the Inca king. The Andean cultures viewed gold and silver as having a different value than that of the Europeans. Tombs were filled with precious stones and belongings of the deceased. Gold was beaten and poured into molds using the "lost wax" method. Platinum and silver were also worked. The Incas, the Aztecs and the Mayas prized colored stones, especially jade and turquoise, and used them to represent water in their jewel work. Red coral and shells were also used.

Stonework

The earliest stonework found was the massive Olmec sculpted heads. Carvings on Maya stelae (carved stone columns), the Aztec stone calendar and their ornate carved gods and goddesses are also examples of carving skill. The precise stonework of the Inca buildings and architectural wonders throughout the New World attest to the Inca, Maya and Aztec excellence with stone.

carved stone stelae

Art Today

The tradition of fine handcrafted objects is prevalent in the Latino world today. Visitors travel to specific parts of Mexico, Central and South America to purchase handsome pottery, masks and other handworked clothing. Christian objects sometimes blend the ancient culture's symbols with today's techniques. Weavings, embroidery, knitted and crocheted linens and clothing are prized by world-famous designers. Papier mache' is the medium for pinatas and figurines. Lacquerware platters, containers and ceramic animal and bird forms are popular with tourists. The silver industry is thriving throughout Mexico. Contemporary designs are displayed with traditional semi precious stones. Souvenirs of many regional holidays are uniquely crafted objects that enhance the celebration.

EASY SALT CLAY PROJECT

EASY SALT CLAY PROJECTS

Materials: cooked baker's clay recipe which includes water, flour, salt and cream of tartar (on page 7), acrylic or tempera paint, cardboard for tree, precut matte frame, glue, knife and modeling tools, box for retablo house and brushes. Pattern is on page 78.

TREE OF LIFE

1. The pattern and cultural information can be found on page 78. Reduce or enlarge the pattern.

2. Trace the tree pattern onto box cardboard, foam core or matte board. Cut with an exacto blade or strong scissors. Paint the tree.

3. Think about your tree objects. The traditional tree has Adam and Eve and the serpent or the Holy Family. Birds, leaves, fruit, angels and flowers are usually depicted. Break off a walnut-sized piece of dough and start molding it. (Keep your dough covered under a protective plastic when it is resting.)

4. Air dry molded objects until they are hard and ready for painting (6-24 hours). Paint bright colors. When paint is dry, arrange objects on the tree and glue to the surface.

A VARIATION ON THE RETABLO

Using a cut up pantry box create your house form with fold-out doors as supports. Add a cut, decorative lintel above the door slotting it to hold. Mold the figures. Use people and creatures that are familiar. Because they are 3-dimensional they should self-support. Paint forms when they are dry.

A DECORATED FRAME

This frame could decorate a mounted mirror or a picture. The production process is the same as for the preceding projects.

Molas

MOLAS

Materials: three sheets of bright colored paper (usually black dominates the colors, next red, then yellow, blue, orange and green), scissors, glue and pencil. Molas can be made from felt pieces as well. These are attached with a needle and thread or a gluing process.

1. Choose three to four different colors of paper. Your top piece will have the main design. Cut it out and lay it on top of the next sheet of paper.

2. Cut out a design as the top piece.

3. Leaving a thin border, cut out the second color around the first shape. Glue the top to the second layer after making your cuts.

4. Now cut out the third shape by laying the two glued shapes on top of the third, cut sheet of paper. Remember to leave a narrow border with each layer. Glue all cut pieces together with their planned thin borders and layers.

5. From the scraps of paper you have left, cut out and glue on details for eyes, ears and mouths.

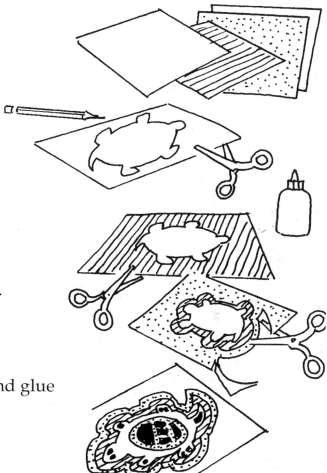

Cuna Indian women of the San Blas Islands near Panama wear their artwork. Blousefronts are decorated with their layered cloth which has been skillfully appliqued with bright contrasting colored cloth. The molas have been an island art form for dozens of years. In the past, natural forms were adapted but today it is not unusual to see a mola with an airplane, a computer keyboard or a soft-drink label.

Huichol Yarn Painting

HUICHOL
YARN PAINTING

Materials: bright colored yarns, glue, scissors, pencil, pre-cut mattes for framing pictures, colored pencils, heavy cardboard squares and novelty matte frames.

1. Draw your design on paper. Color it with colored pencils or crayons that correspond with your yarn choices.

2. When you are ready to work with your surface, squeeze some glue onto your cardboard form.

3. Stick your strand of yarn to it. Work in small sections so the glue does not dry before you stick your yarn to it.

4. Press the yarn firmly into the dried glue section. Pack yarn strands tightly together. Snip ends with scissors.

5. Make a yarn outline around your design with a double row of contrasting yarn. Fill in the background with a final color. The background color will surround your design.

The Huichol Indians in the remote sections of Mexico's Nayarit mountains create these yarn painting as votive offerings. They are also successful folk art items. Traditionally, a wood surface is covered with a mixture of beeswax and petroleum jelly. The sun warms the surface.

The design is scratched into the wax. The soft yarn strands are pressed into the wax surface. Designs and colors are rich in symbolic meaning. Religion and art are bound together. Zigzag lines represent snakes and are a prayer for rain.

BALEROS AND CASCARONES

BALEROS AND CASCARONES

Materials: manila folder or posterboard for the cone, yarn or string, masking tape, paint or markers, tissue paper, stapler, scissors, bead and hollow egg.

THE BALERO is a universal game. The player attempts to catch the ball in the cone.

1. Cut your cone 11 inches on the side, 14 inches on top. Curve the top and punch a hole in the middle.

2. Decorate the flat cone in a bright, festive way.

3. Staple the sides and bottom tip of cone. Cut the string about 24-36" long and attach a bead with a secure knot.

CASCARONES are confetti-filled hollow eggs nestled in a flamboyantly decorated cone. At the high point of the fiesta, guests "bonk" a favorite person on the head and the broken egg releases clouds of confetti.

1. Blow out the inside of a fresh egg and let the hollow egg dry upside down overnight.

2. Fill it with prepared confetti. Cover the blow hole with masking tape. Decorate the egg with markers.

3. Prepare the cone as you did for the bolero game. Decorate this cone with layered fringes of tissue paper. Make a thin line of glue along the top inside of the cone. Fit the egg into the decorated cone with the glue securing it.

The eighteen month solar year of the Aztecs had a series of festivals described by the Spanish historians as rich in flowers and pageantry. These might be lighthearted vestiges of the great events dedicated to earth, sun, water, fire and corn.

Amate

AMATE

Materials: a brown paper bag, scissors, pencil, appropriate paper for mounting, glue and ribbon.

1. Choose a symmetrical design. Fold brown paper in half. Hold in place with paper clips.

2. Starting at fold draw half of your design. Cut it out. Unfold and open.

3. Determine whether your amate design will be displayed on a greeting card, on a wall, as a framed picture or as a book cover. There may be many other ways to use your amate.

4. Carefully glue the back of your cutout and mount it on paper.

These paper cutouts from the bark of the amate (uh mah tay) tree are made by the Otomi Indians of Mexico. The subjects for these symmetrical designs are usually plant forms, birds and animals. They are used for magical purposes in an effort to control nature, protect crops, rid a place of evil and guard the home. Bark paper was used by the Maya in making their elaborate codex records.

PAPER AND TIN FOR A FIESTA

PAPER AND TIN FOR A FIESTA

*Materials: brightly colored tissue paper, scissors, tin cans, nail and hammer,
glue, string and spray paint (optional).*

FESTIVE PAPER CUTS

These accordian folded tissue paper
cut "doilies" are traditionally strung
across a room or narrow street.

1. Decide on the size of your tissue paper
square. Cut your colored papers to this size.

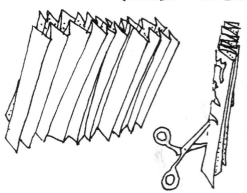

2. Fold into 1 to 1 1/2 inch folds. You might combine
more than one paper for mass production. Paper clips
at the top will hold the layers in place.

3. Cut shapes, designs, etc. along the folds. A string
is inserted across a glued hem with the bright lacy
tissue paper squares lined up, one after another.

LUMINARIAS

Feliz Navidad (Christmas) and other important
celebrations often feature rooflines and wall tops
alight with glowing paper bags. They hold enough
sand for weight and a votive candle. Often cut
designs give a patterned look to the light. Sturdier
and also effective are tin cans that have been punched
with ancient designs and sprayed a festive color.

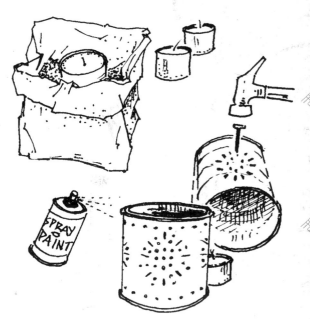

1. Save your empty cans, the bigger the better. Fill
with water and freeze. Draw your design on a paper
strip and tape it around the can. Rest the can on a
folded towel between your legs. With a nail and a
hammer punch the paper design into the can with
holes, slits, etc.

2. Spray paint the can exterior to enhance the design.

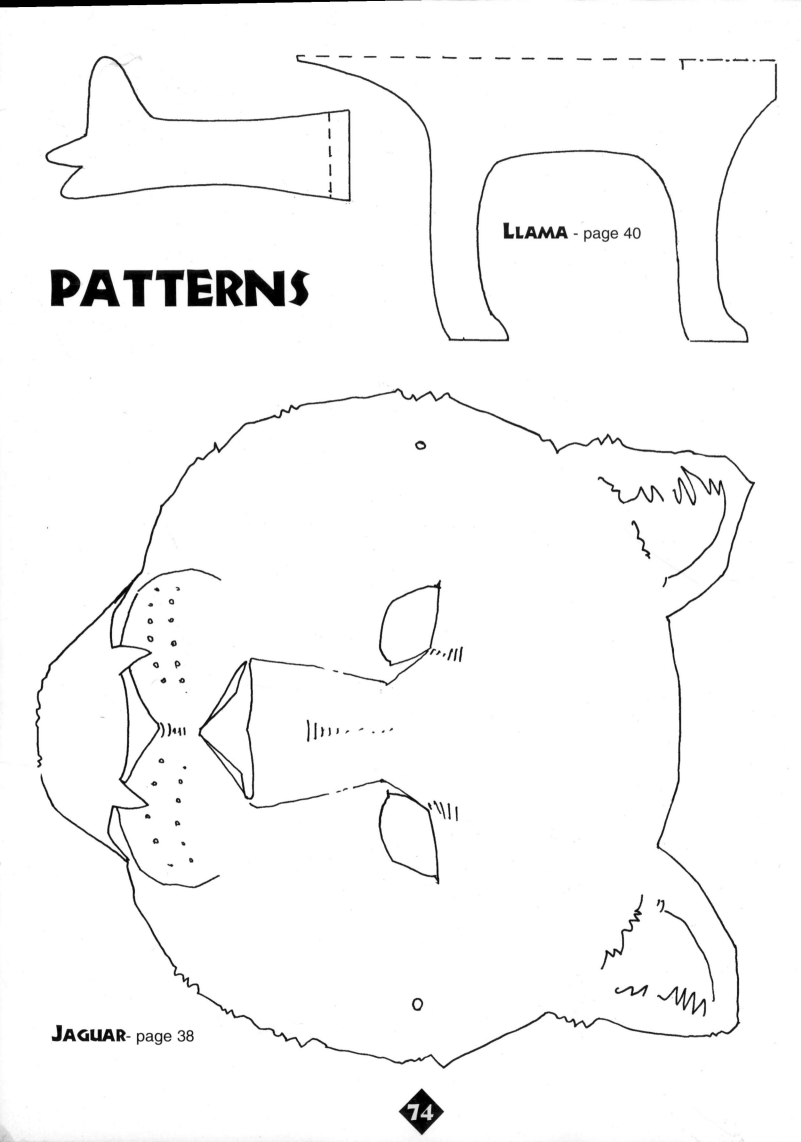

PATTERNS

LLAMA - page 40

JAGUAR - page 38

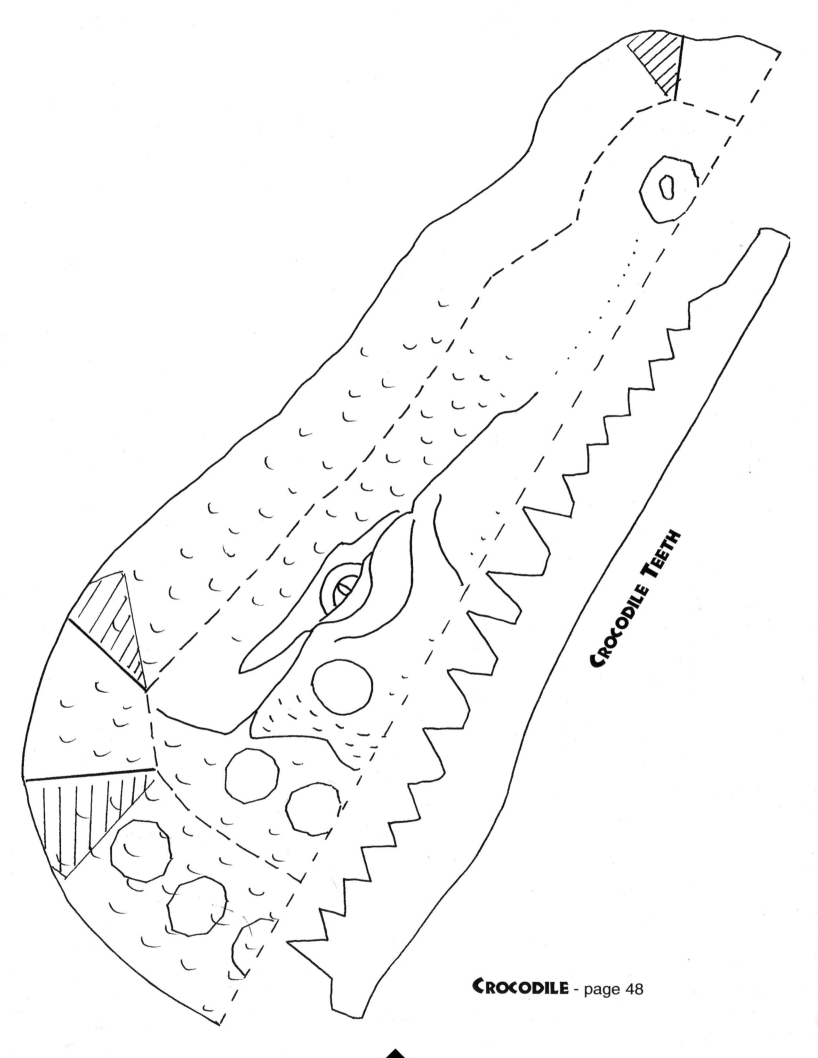

CROCODILE TEETH

CROCODILE - page 48

THE EYE OF GOD (continued from pages 14 and 15).

The god's eye or *tsikuri* originated with the Huichol Indians and is a way of communicating with deities. The diamond shape is a form through which the gods view the people, keeping them in health and protecting them from harm. Ojo de dios have a special association with children, and fathers dedicate them to gods on behalf of small sons and daughters. There may be many "eyes" with each signifying a child's year: two eyes counting as two years, etc.

MOSAIC MASK - page 43
GOLD MASK - page 47

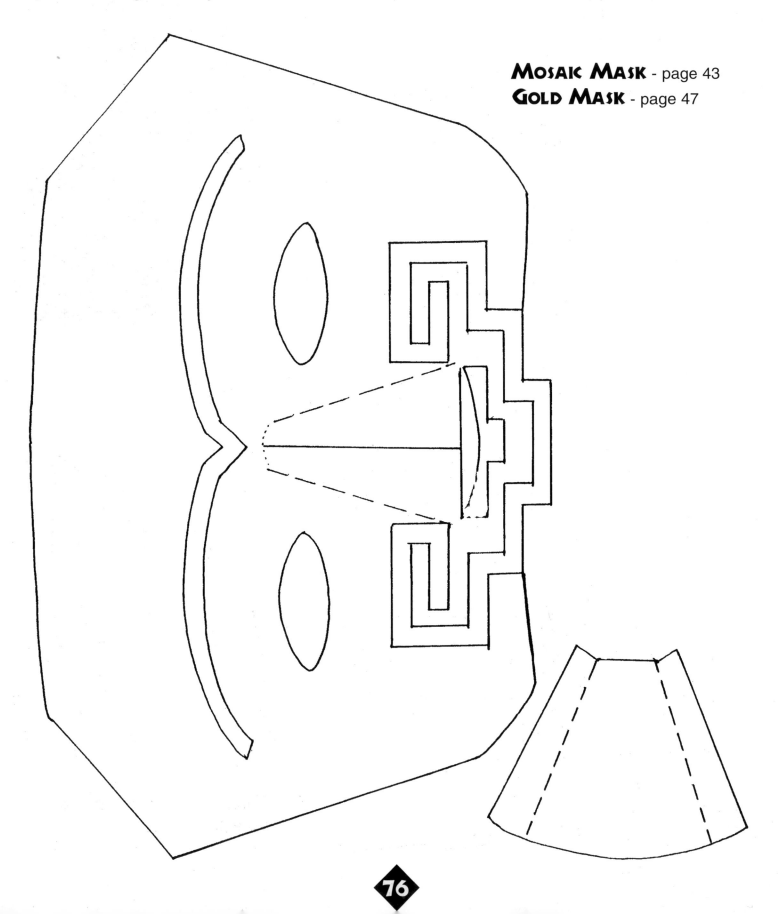

Jade Clay and Paper Mosaic Mask

(continued from page 42)

1. Make the cooked salt clay as described on page 7. Add green food coloring to most of your dough. Roll out your dough as thinly as possible. Cut into 1/2 inch squares. Some of the squares will be painted brown. Let your mosaic pieces air-dry. Allow 12 to 18 hours to dry.

2. Glue the mosaic squares onto the cardboard mask. The mask can be painted first. Look at the photo of the mosaic mask. The contrasting brown tiles are optional.

This mask is a replica of a heavy jade artifact that was made to rest on the head section of the corpse of an important figure.

Jade Paper Mosaic Mask

1. Prepare your spattered jade paper as described on page 7.
2. Cut the jade and coral paper into squares of 1/2 inch. The squares do not have to be perfect.
3. Glue the cut squares to your cardboard mask pattern. Cut out the eyes if the mask is to be worn.

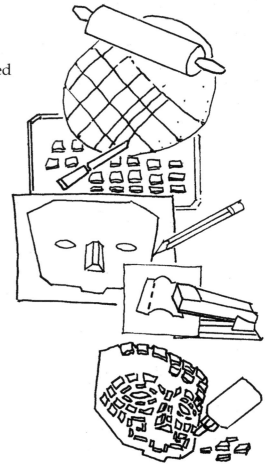

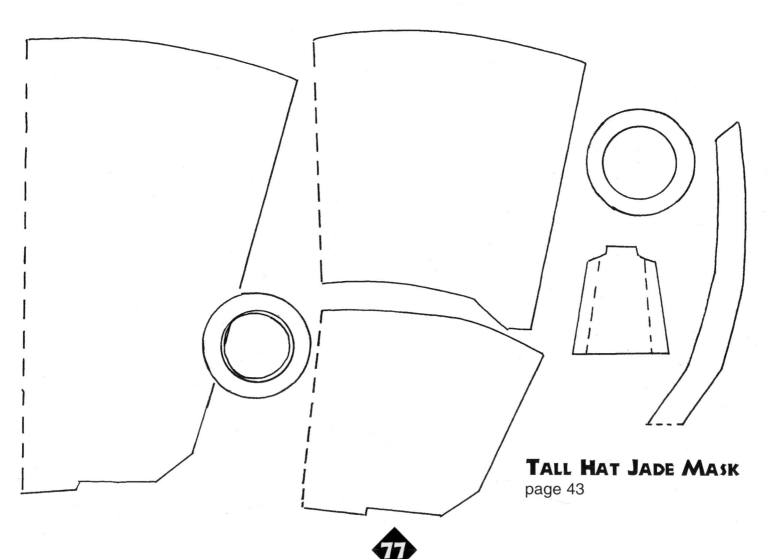

Tall Hat Jade Mask
page 43

77

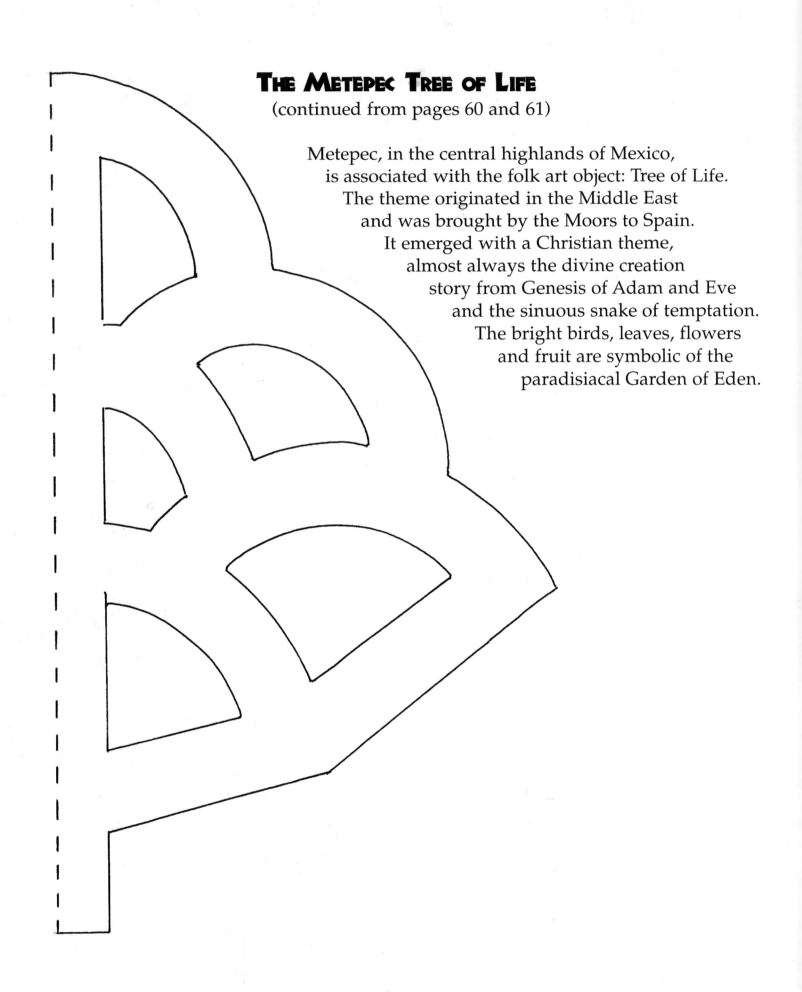

THE METEPEC TREE OF LIFE

(continued from pages 60 and 61)

Metepec, in the central highlands of Mexico,
is associated with the folk art object: Tree of Life.
The theme originated in the Middle East
and was brought by the Moors to Spain.
It emerged with a Christian theme,
almost always the divine creation
story from Genesis of Adam and Eve
and the sinuous snake of temptation.
The bright birds, leaves, flowers
and fruit are symbolic of the
paradisiacal Garden of Eden.

THE MAYA

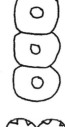

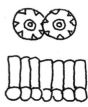

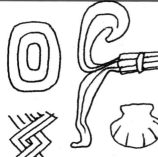

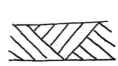

THE AZTECS

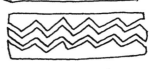

THE INCA

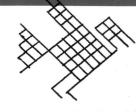

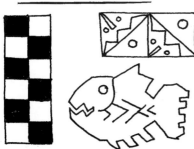

79

INDEX

ACKNOWLEDGMENTS

Dr. Robert A. Rees,
at the time with UCLA Extension, is credited with giving me the opportunity
to research and refine the ideas and information in this book.

Several professionals reviewed this manuscript and gave input:

Emily Merrill Mortensen
edited and reviewed the text from its first rough draft. Emily previewed the crafts and
choice of materials, working with her three daughters as the best judges of all.

Judy Hansen
edited the early copy.

Jocelyn Young
reviewed the text for editing errors and general context.

Kay Jones
one of Salt Lake City's most versatile art teachers in the realm of folk art,
is always willing to try concepts in her classroom and offer suggestions on materials.
The faculties at her various schools were helpful advisers as well.

Ray and Marilyn Anderson
loaned some of the objects photographed on the double pages and the crafts from their
personal collection gathered from living and traveling in Peru, Chile, Bolivia and Ecuador.

Anne Dalgleish Bell
shared her treasures and wealth of information on each carefully offered item.

Donna Mack
owner of the remarkable folk art store, One People, in Anchorage, Alaska
provided the items for the double page photo on pages 30 and 31.

Javed Chowdhury
computer specialist, assisted with the initial graphic work.

Madlyn Tanner
edited the final copy.

BIBLIOGRAPHY

Baquedano, Elizabeth, *Aztec, Inca & Maya*, New York, Eyewitness Books, Alfred A Knopf, 1993.

Miller, Rebecca Stone, *Art of the Andes from Chavin to Inca*, London, Thames and Hudson, 1995.

Glassie, Henry, *The Spirit of Folk Art: the Girard Collection at the Museum of International Folk Art*, New York, Harry N. Abrams, Inc., 1989.

Sayer, Chloe, *Crafts of Mexico, New York, Doubleday and Company, Inc., 1977.*

Stuart, George and Gene S., *The Mysterious Maya*, Washington, D.C., National Geographic Society, 1983.

Enciso, Jorge, *Design Motifs of Ancient Mexico*, New York, Dover Publications, Inc., 1953.

Stuart, Gene, *America's Ancient Cities*, Washington D.C. National Geographic Society, 1988.

Boltin, Lee and Douglas Newton, *Masterpieces of Primitive Art*, New York, Alfred A. Knopf, 1978.

Leonard, Jonathan Norton, *Great Ages of Man: Ancient America, A History of the World's Cultures*, Time-Life Books, New York, Time Incorporated, 1967.

Gardner, Joseph L., *The Mysteries of the Ancient Americas: The New World before Columbus*, Pleasantville, New York, Reader's Digest Association, Inc., 1986.

Schele, Linda and David Freidel, *A Forest of Kings: The Untold Story of the Ancient Maya*, New York, Quill William Morrow, 1990.

Franch, Jose Alcina, *Pre-Columbian Art*, New York, Harry N. Abrams, Inc., 1983.

Lothrop, S.K., *Treasures of Ancient America: The Arts of the Pre-Columbian Civilizations from Mexico to Peru*, Geneva, Skira Publications, 1964.

Caso, Alfonso, *The Aztecs, People of the Sun*, Norman, Oklahoma, University of Oklahoma Press, 1958.

Swanson, Earl H., Warwick Bray, Ian Farrington, *The Ancient Americas*, New York, Peteer Bedrick Books, 1975.

Viva los Artesanos! Catalog of an exhibit celebrating Mexican folk art from the collection of Fred and Barbara Meiers, published by the Folk Art Museum of Cultural History, Los Angeles, California.

CENTRAL AND SOUTH AMERICA

FOOD CONTRIBUTIONS

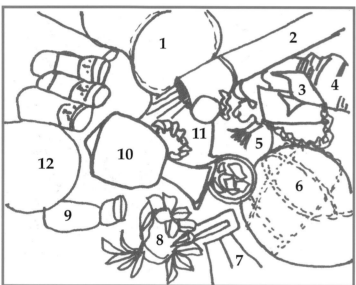

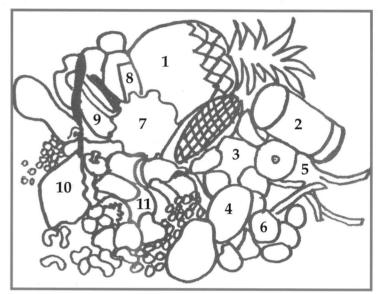

1. Chilean Basket
2. Quiver with arrows used for small mammal hunting. The tip is poison-dipped.
3. Carved bird from Mexico
4. Woven hat from Bolivia
5. Bronze stirrup from Conquistador period
6. Gourd with strung pod covering. When it is shaken it is a percussion instrument.
7. Woven Inca design in alpaca yarn from Peru
8. A rattle made of hooves from Guatemala
9. Replicated Peruvian doll. The originals were discovered in burial sites.
10. An aryballo shaped jar from Peru. This is the jar that contains fermenting beverages. It is stored upside down.
11. Ancient whorls, used in spinning and the indigenous weaving industry.
12. A gourd, shaped to be a bowl, with incised patterns that have been rubbed with pigment.

1. pineapple
2. coffee
3. tomato
4. avocado
5. string beans
6. potatoes
7. squash
8. cinnamon
9. vanilla
10. chocolate
11. papaya
12. cashews
13 beans
14. nutmeg
15. peanuts
17. peppers
18. nutmeg
19. corn

ART TODAY

1. Mayan design on clay plaque
2. Knitted doll from Ecuador
3. Tourist doll from Colombia
4. Clay duck container from Acapulco, Mexico
5. Candlestick from Izucar de Matamoros in Mexico
6. Carved duck from Ixtapan de la Sal in Mexico
7. Woven sandal
8. Painted box from Tonala. The clay is called *aromatic clay.*
9. Double candle holder from Oaxaca, Mexico
10. Fanciful animals inspired by the fantasy creatures created by the Linares family in Mexico City.
11. Silver from Taxco, Mexico
12. Tile and silver mirror from Puebla, Mexico
13. Clay dish from Mazatlan

FOLK ART

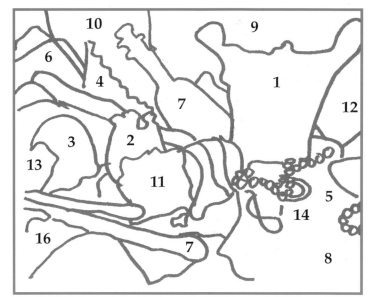

1. Jaguar head mask
2. A clay whistle depicting a circle of figures
3. Snake patterned clay mask
4. Panpipes made of bamboo from Peru
5. Silver worked jewelry which reflects the Spanish skill with metal
6. Embroidered clothing
7. Huichol beaded figures
8. Red Bolivian shawl
9. Ecuadorian woven piece
10. Mexican woven yardage
11. Carved jaguar
12. Huichol cross-stitched bag
13. Transformation mask of a fish
14. Ecuadorian straw ball necklace
15. Leather braided sandal
16. Mola from the Cuna Indians

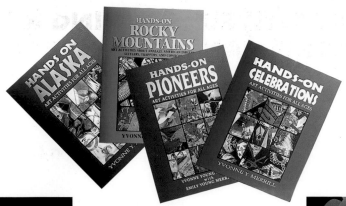

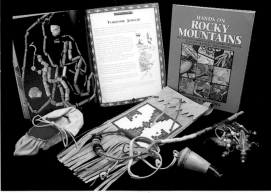

Hands-on Rocky Mountains
(ISBN 0-9643177-2-9)

Books from
KITS
PUBLISHING

Yvonne Merrill's activity books are not typical of what is usually available. A full-color photograph of each craft is featured, often with an authentic artifact about that art activity. The authenticity is further insured with cultural facts, easy-to-follow directions and illustrated background information. Libraries, teachers, home-schoolers, museums and parents will want to own this hands-on series.

Hands-on Celebrations
(ISBN 0-9643177-4-5)

Hands-on Pioneers
(ISBN 1-57345-085-5)

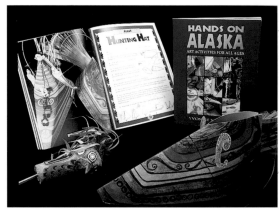

Hands-on Alaska
(ISBN 0-9643177-3-7)

ORDER FORM

SEND TO:_____ PO # _____

ADDRESS:_____

CITY:_____ STATE:_____ ZIP_____

CONTACT NAME: _____ PHONE: _____

HOW DID YOU HEAR ABOUT THESE BOOKS?

❐ ____ Hands-on Latin America
❐ ____ Hands-on Rocky Mountains
❐ ____ Hands-on Pioneers
❐ ____ Hands-on Celebrations
❐ ____ Hands-on Alaska

_____ Total Quantity Ordered
_____ Shipping and Handling
_____ Total Enclosed/PO

Books are $20⁰⁰ each.
Shipping and Handling - $3⁰⁰ for the first book
and $1⁰⁰ for each additional book.
All books shipped book rate unless otherwise requested.

Make checks payable to:
KITS PUBLISHING
2359 E. Bryan Avenue
Salt Lake City, Utah 84108
Toll free: 1-888-581-2517   fax: (801) 582-2540
e-mail: info@hands-on.com   http://www.hands-on.com

INTEGRATED LEARNING KITS
ART EDUCATION AND MULTICULTURAL UNITS

These programs are in-depth tools for the institution that does not have art teachers or Latino studies curriculum. These kits have been field-tested successfully and emphasize art production and integrated disciplines.

COLOR

- Science of color
- Nature of color
- Creative Expression of color
- Art Appreciation
- Art Production

FORM/SHAPE

- Geometry art
- Architecture
- Art Appreciation: Cubists, sculpture
- Art Production

TEXTURE

- Science and Texture
- Creative Expression
- Nature and Texture
- Art Appreciation
- Art Production

DESIGN

- Creative Expression
- Nature and Design
- Science of pattern
- Art Appreciation
- Art Production

These photos show a partial selection of the kits contents.

THE LATIN AMERICAN KIT

- The geography of Mexico, Central America, Caribbean and South America
- The Maya, Incas and Aztecs
- The natural world
- The great people of yesterday and today in history, cultural expression and contributions
- A focus on each country

These kits are $1,500 each and require a 12 hour on-site-training session. Kits have been museum and classroom tested. For more information, contact kit developer, **Yvonne Merrill:**
Toll free at 1-888-581-2517   fax - 1-801-582-2540
email: info@hands-on.com   http://www.hands-on.com

J
745.
5
MER

Merrill, Yvonne
Young.

Hands-on Latin
America.

32827009197797
$20.00   12/02/1998

DATE			
2/99	i	8/99	✓